# CRAFTY IDEAS WITH

# FABRICS

## Melanie Rice

Illustrated by Lynne Farmer

Photography by Chris Fairclough

**HODDER AND STOUGHTON**
LONDON   SYDNEY   AUCKLAND   TORONTO

To Chris, Catherine and Alex,
for all their help.

British Library Cataloguing in Publication Data

Rice, Melanie
    Crafty ideas with fabrics.
    1. Handicrafts using fabrics. Annuals
    I. Title
    746

    ISBN 0-340-50107-3

First published 1989

Published by Hodder and Stoughton Children's Books,
a division of Hodder and Stoughton Ltd,
Mill Road, Dunton Green, Sevenoaks, Kent TN13 2YA

Design by Sally Boothroyd

Cover illustration by Lynn Breeze

Book list compiled by Peter Bone, Senior Librarian,
Children's and Schools Services, Hampshire County Library

Printed in Italy

# CONTENTS

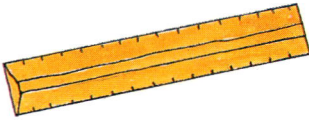

# Note to parents and teachers

All the ideas in this book are easy to carry out at home or at school. Every item has been made by my own young children and then photographed for this book. Each page has clear instructions accompanied by numbered, easy-to-follow illustrations.

For some of the items I used material from my rag-bag; for others pieces of old sheet and even old clothes (T-shirts, cotton shirts and shorts for example). Choose materials that do not fray easily. Squares of felt, embroidery silks and pipe-cleaners can be bought from craft shops or department stores. Bamboo canes are usually available from flower shops.

For activities involving dyes, you will need to find an old bucket and an old wooden spoon, as well as a space to hang the finished items to dry. I bought cold water dyes and packets of fixative to stop the dyes washing out.

To stick materials together use a clear fabric adhesive, or PVA adhesive which is just as good.

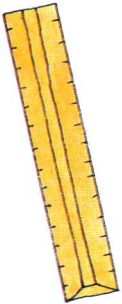

## Note to children

**Things to remember:**

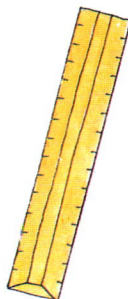

1 Read all the instructions carefully before you begin so that you know what you have to do. Use the illustrations to help you.

2 Make sure everything you need is ready before you start.

3 Spread newspaper over your working surface – this is especially important for messy projects.

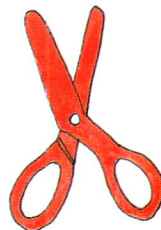

4 Clean up any mess when you have finished.

5 Put everything away tidily.

At the end of each project I have suggested other things for you to try to make. Maybe you have some ideas of your own. Don't be afraid to try them out.

Melanie Rice

# SHIELD

You can hang this shield on your bedroom door. Like a family coat of arms, it tells people something about the owner.

## You will need:

bamboo cane (30cm)
glue
large piece of material
  (25cm × 35cm)
smaller pieces of material
paper
pencil
scissors

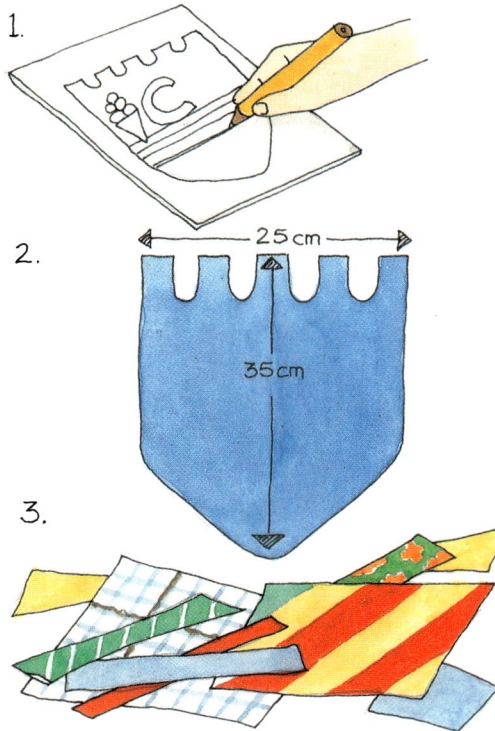

1. 

2. 

3. 

**1**  Draw a design for your shield on a piece of paper. Work out a design that tells everyone about yourself – for example, your hobbies, your favourite foods, your initials, etc.

**2**  Choose a large piece of plain-coloured material for the background and cut it into the shape shown.

**3**  Pick out a number of contrasting pieces of material (ones that will show up well against the background) to make your design.

4.

**4** Using a pencil, draw outlines of different pictures on to these smaller pieces of material.

**5** Cut out the shapes and arrange them on the shield. Stick them in place.

**6** Fold the top edge of the shield over a cane, as shown, and stick down firmly.

5.

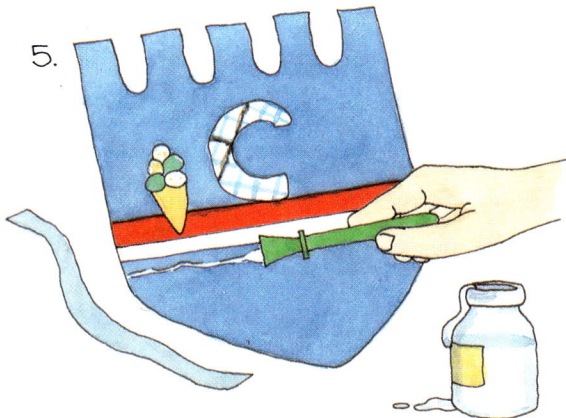

6.

## Protect your favourite book with a strong fabric cover.

**1** Place the open book on the wrong side of the fabric. Cut along the dotted lines.

**2** Fold over the edges and stitch as shown.

**3** Decorate the front with a collage made from scraps of left-over material.

1.

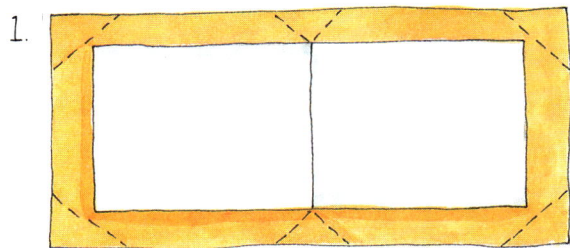

2.

3.

# THE ODDS AND EVENS GAME

This very simple game is quick to make and fun to play. You can design some different boards for the frogs to jump around.

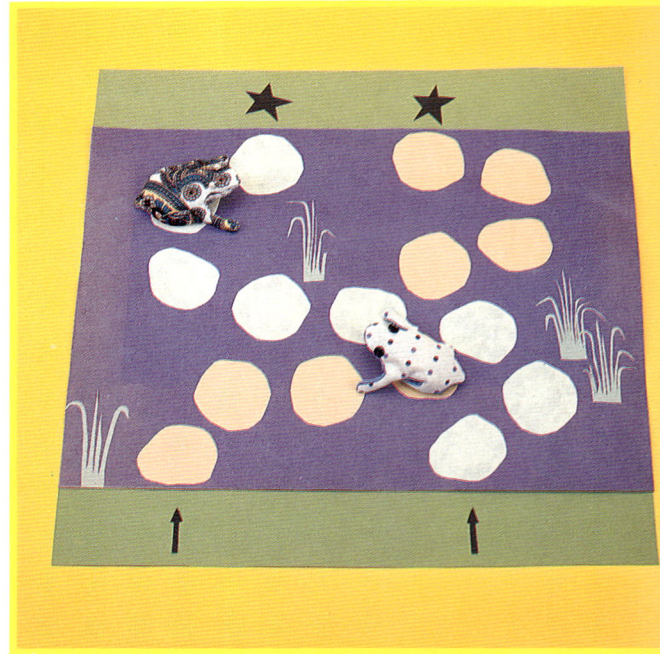

## You will need:

| | |
|---|---|
| 4 buttons | needle |
| card (50cm × 50cm) | paint |
| coloured paper | paper |
| cotton | pencil |
| dice | pins |
| 4 pieces of material | scissors |
| (15cm × 15cm) | split peas |

1.

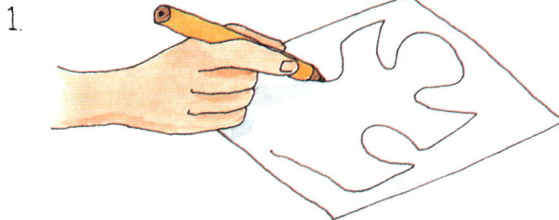

**1** Draw and cut out the frog shape from a piece of paper.

2.

**2** Place one piece of material on top of another and pin the frog to them. Cut around the frog.

3.

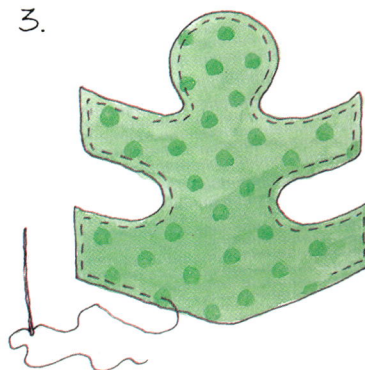

**3** Put the right sides of the material together and stitch around the edge of the shape, leaving a gap by the tail as shown.

**4** Turn the frog the right way out and fill with split peas. Then sew up the hole.

**5** Sew on two buttons as eyes. Make another frog in the same way.

**6** Paint a blue river on the card.

**7** Using coloured paper, cut out rows of stepping-stones and stick them on to the card, crossing the river.

### To play

The object is to jump the frogs across the river. Take turns to throw the dice. One frog moves each time its 'owner' throws an even number, the other moves when its 'owner' throws an odd number. A frog may only jump one stone at a time. The winner is the first frog across the river.

Other bean-bag animals can be made in this way.

To make a mouse you will also need two circles of felt for its ears, thick threads for its whiskers and fur fabric and string for its tail.

# TIE AND DYE SCARF

Tie and dye is a quick, simple way to make patterns on fabric. It is practised all over the world. Sling the scarves round your neck, or tie at the waist.

**You will need:**

old bucket
length of cotton material
cold water dye
fixative
pebbles or marbles
scissors
stick
string

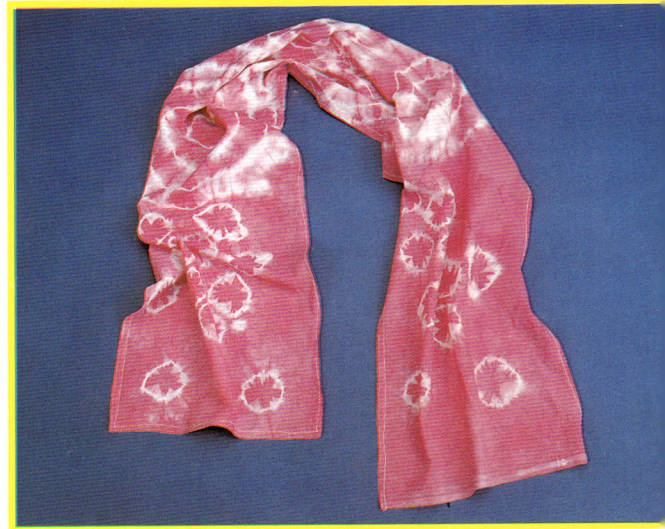

1  Take a scarf-length piece of cotton (a piece from an old sheet is fine).

2  Tie the scarf in one, or several of these ways
   - tie a pebble or marble into the cotton (A)
   - twist the cotton round, then tie it in several places as shown (B)
   - pleat the material and tie (C).

   Be sure that all your ties are tight.

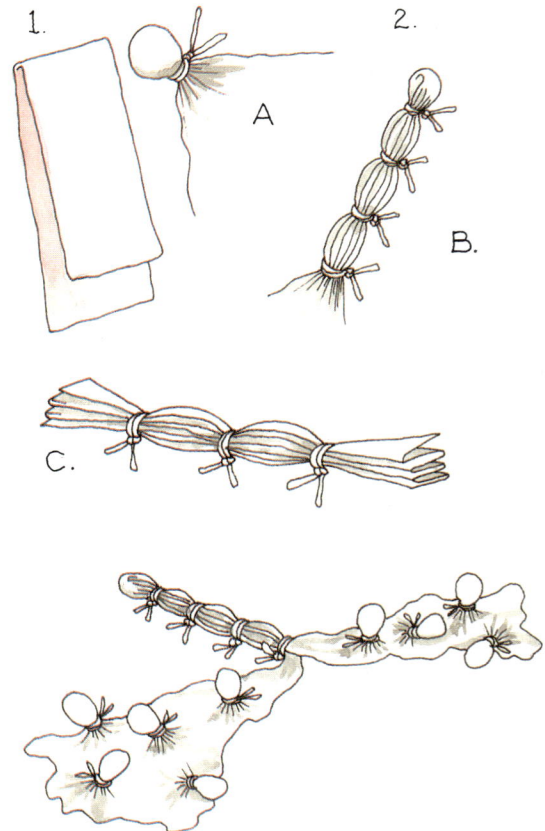

**3** Mix the dye, following the instructions on the packet. Add a fixative so the colour does not wash out.

**4** Put the scarf into the dye and leave until the colour is twice as dark as you want.

**5** Rinse thoroughly in cold water.

**6** Leave to dry, then remove the ties.

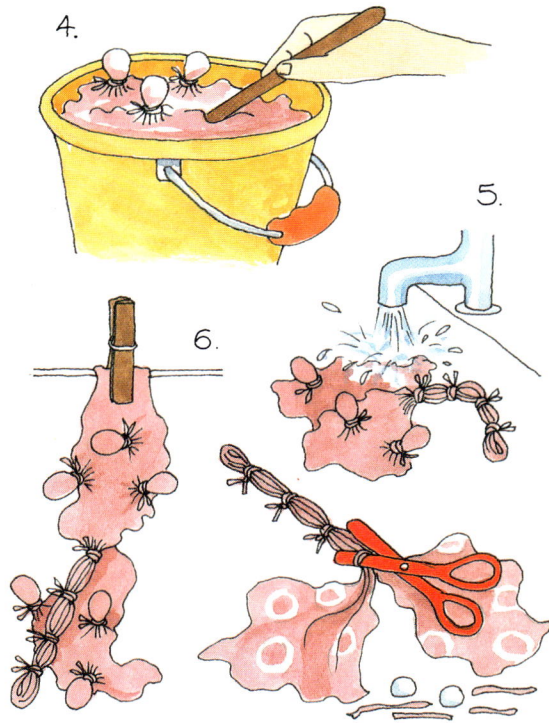

**7** This process can be repeated with a second, darker colour.

Old cotton shirts and skirts can be given a new lease of life with tie and dye.

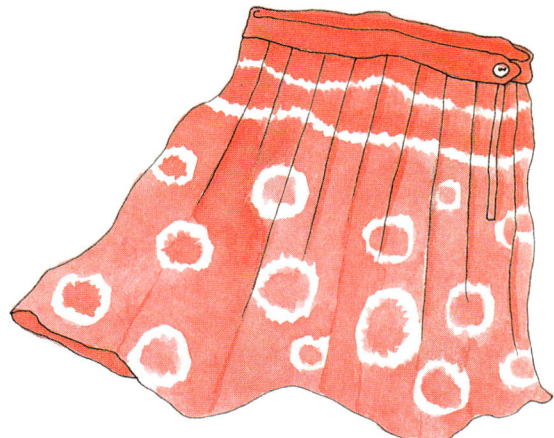

# PIPE-CLEANER DOLLS

Make one, two or a whole team of dolls and bend them into action poses.

## For each doll you will need:

cotton
felt or other material
felt pens
needle
3 pipe-cleaners
styrofoam (found in craft shops)
   or papier mâché ball
wool

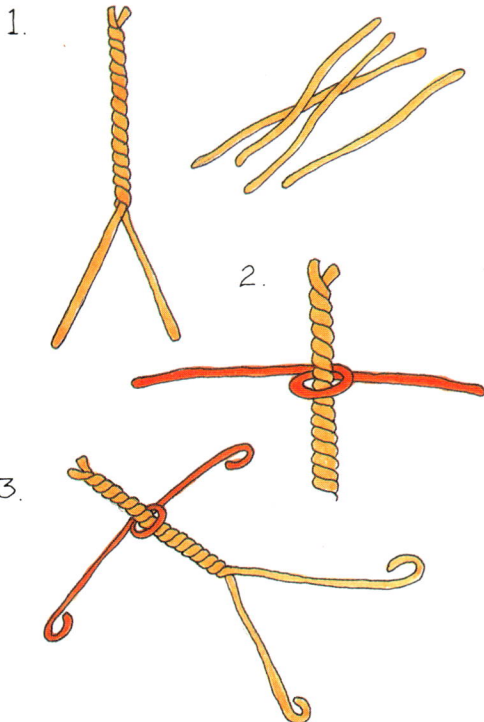

1. **1** Twist the tops of two pipe-cleaners together as shown.

**2** Wrap the third pipe-cleaner round them to make arms.

**3** Bend the ends of the arms and legs to make hands and feet.

**4** Cut a rectangle of felt. Fold in half and cut a triangle from the top. Sew three quarters of the way up each side as shown.

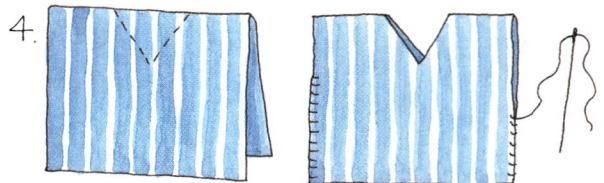

5.

**5** Cut two pieces of felt in the shape of shorts. Sew up the sides as shown.

6.

**6** Put the clothes on the doll and stitch the trousers to the shirt.

7.

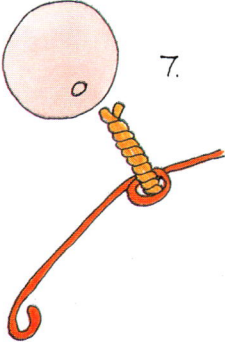

**7** Make a small hole in the ball and stick on top of the body.

8.

**8** Cut scraps of wool and glue to the head, then draw on a face.

Pipe-cleaner figures can also be made to illustrate stories.

# WOVEN BRACELET

Indian children make bracelets like this one by weaving brightly coloured strands of string or wool.

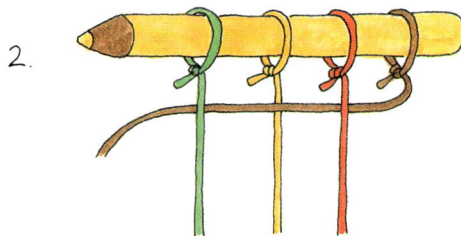

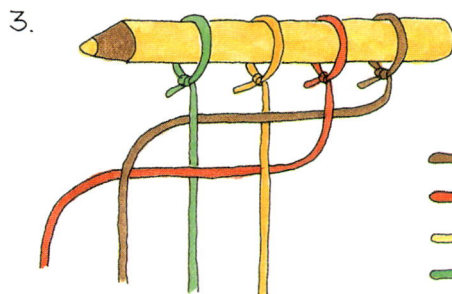

1. **1** Tie four pieces of wool, each about 30cm long, round a pencil as shown.

2. **2** Take the right-hand strand and weave through the others.

3. **3** Now take the new right-hand strand and weave through the others as shown.

4. **4** Continue weaving in this way until you have a band long enough to go round your wrist.

**5.**

**6.**

**7.**

**8.**

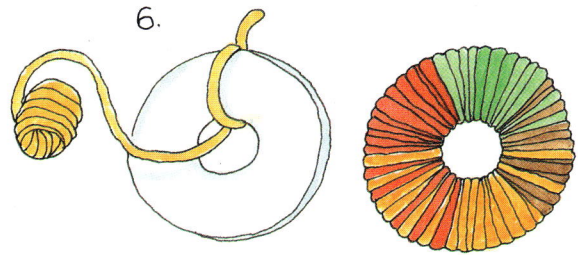

**5** Tie the ends together. Remove the pencil and thread another piece of wool through the loops. Tie firmly to prevent the weaving coming undone.

**6** Make a small woolly ball by cutting two rings of card as shown. Hold together and wrap in wool.

**7** Cut the wool between the two pieces of card. Tie a piece of wool round the middle and remove the card.

**8** Hang a ball from either end of the bracelet.

---

More woven jewellery.

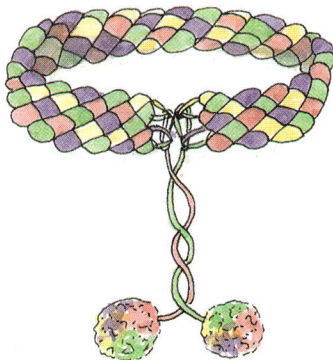

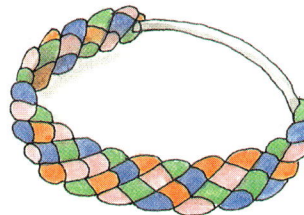

You can make pendants and headbands too.

# BATIK SHORTS

Batik is a way of painting designs on to material with wax. It is found in many regions of the world, and especially in Indonesia.

CAUTION: Melting wax can be dangerous. Ask an adult to help you make this.

1.

**1** Melt two wax crayons of one colour in the saucepan, then drip the hot wax on to the shorts using a wooden spoon. Repeat with the second colour.

**2** Mix a cold water dye in the bucket, following the instructions on the tin. Add some fixative so the dye will not wash out.

**3** Soak the shorts in the dye until they are a darker shade than you want, then rinse well in clear water.

**4** Leave to dry.

**5** Place two sheets of newspaper, or other absorbent paper, under the shorts, two inside and two on top. Now iron the shorts. The newspaper will soak up the wax as the iron melts it. Put in clean sheets of newspaper and continue ironing until no more wax comes out.

Make a cushion cover by sewing together two squares of batik material.

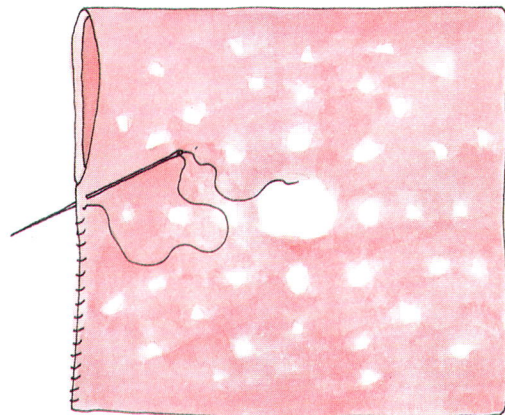

# BOUNCING DOLL

This cuddly little doll will spring to life if you hold her by her hat elastic and jig her up and down.

**You will need:**

2 pieces of card (15cm × 15cm)
cotton
round elastic (90cm)
material
needle
pencil
scissors
stuffing

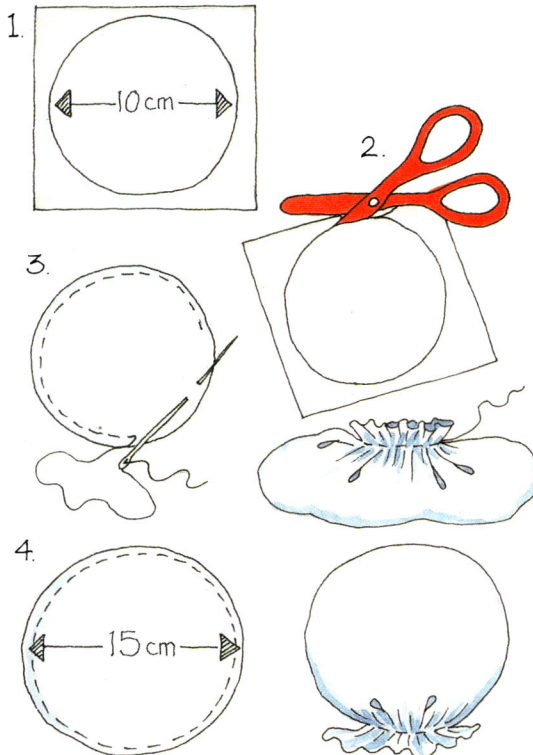

1. 
2. 
3. 
4. 

**1** Cut out a circle of card about 10cm in diameter.

**2** Cut out 46 circles of material using the card as a template.

**3** Using running stitches, sew round the edge of the first circle of the material. Pull the thread tight to gather into the middle and fasten. Repeat with the other circles.

**4** Cut out another circle, about 15cm in diameter. Gather it up in the same way, but before fastening, fill with stuffing to make a head.

**5** Cut out a triangle of material, with 8cm sides. Fold in half and stitch the side as shown to make a hat.

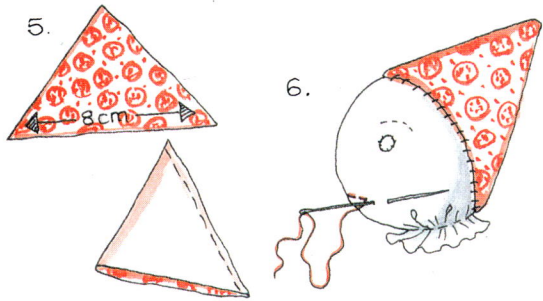

**6** Sew or stick the hat to the head, and sew on a mouth and eyes.

**7** Cut 3 pieces of elastic about 30cm long. Thread 20 of the circles on to one piece (A). Tie a knot at both ends. Thread 16 circles onto the second piece (B) and knot at both ends.

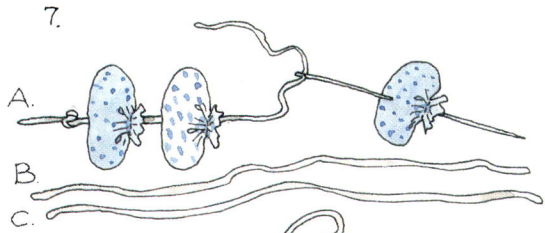

**8** Tie the third piece of elastic (C) half way along line A. Thread on 9 of the remaining circles then tie half way along line B as shown. Thread elastic C through the remaining circle, then up through the head and hat. Tie with a loop at the top.

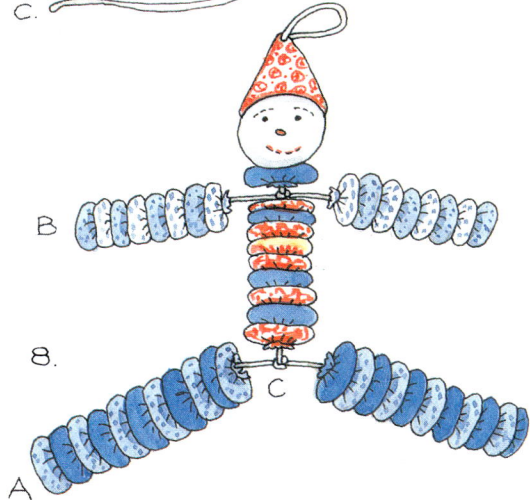

Circles can be joined together to make snakes and giraffes. You might think of other animals as well.

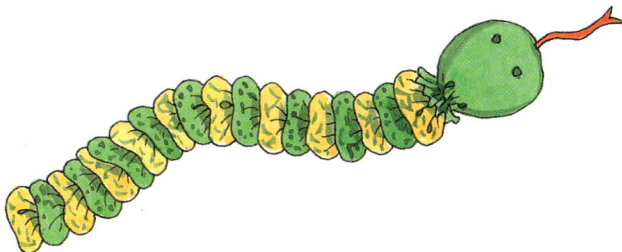

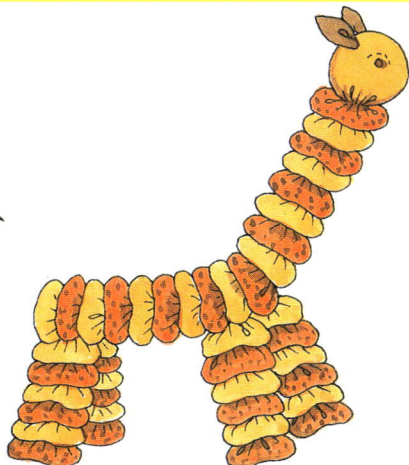

# GREETINGS CARDS

Send cards with a difference this year. They can only be made by hand, so you rarely see anything like them in shops.

**You will need:**

card (24cm × 16cm)
embroidery silks
felt pens
needle
pencil
ruler
scissors

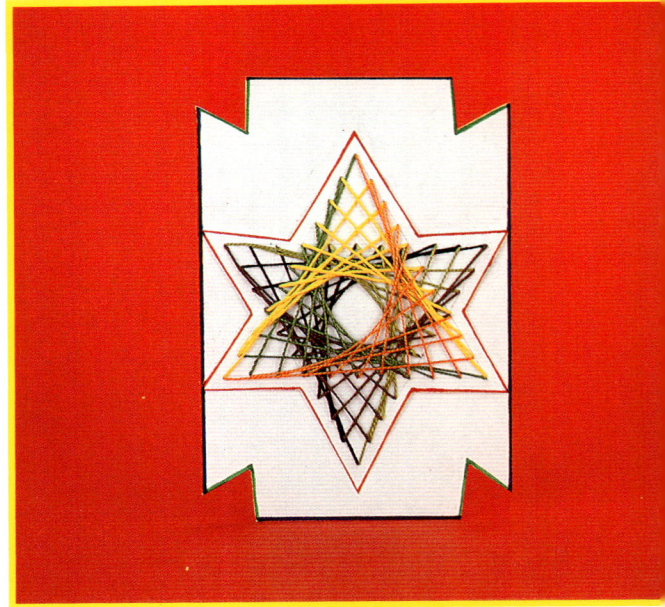

1.

16 cm

24 cm

2.

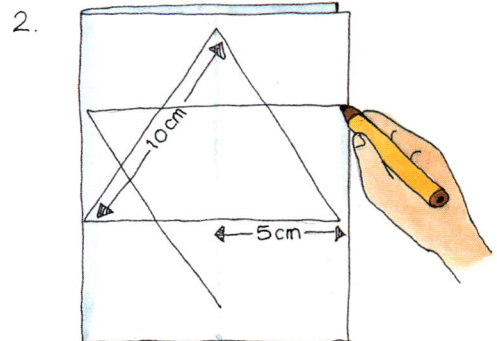

10 cm

5 cm

3.

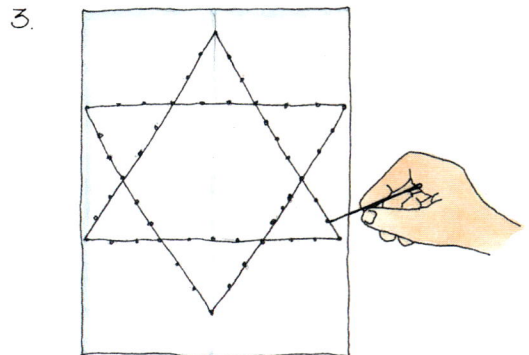

**1** Take a piece of card, 24cm by 16cm, and fold in half.

**2** Draw a faint pencil line down the middle, then draw two triangles of the measurements shown.

**3** Mark 1cm intervals along the edges of the triangles. Prick a hole at each mark with a needle.

**4** To sew the top triangle: thread a piece of silk up through the top hole (A) and down through (B), then up through (C) and down through (D). Continue this pattern as shown. Repeat, using a different coloured thread, for the other sides.

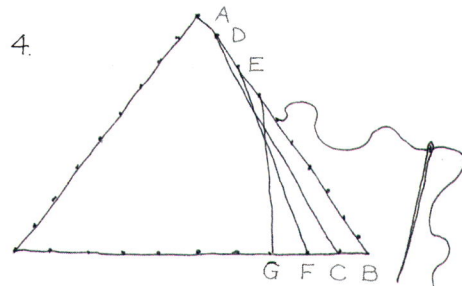

**5** To sew the bottom triangle: follow the instructions in 4 above, using contrasting coloured threads.

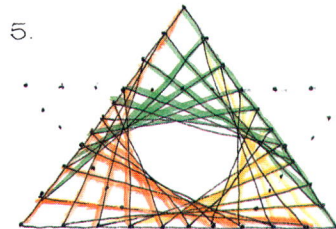

**6** Open the card and stick a piece of paper over the back of the design, to cover loose ends.

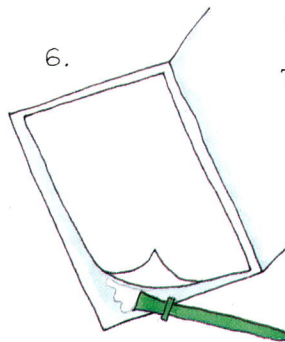

**7** Cut the card into an interesting shape and write on your message.

Here are some other designs you can try sewing.

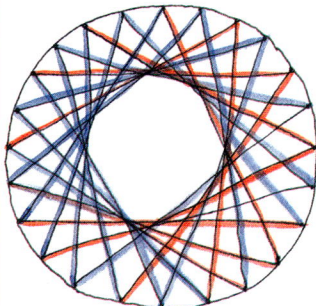

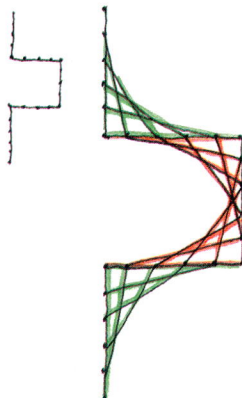

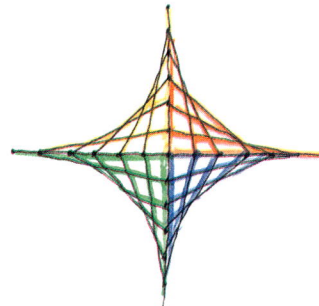

# DESK TIDY

Collect all your pens and pencils together in one special holder, decorated in Mexican style.

1–2.

3.

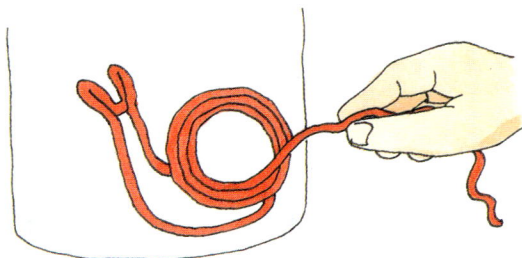

1 Paste some glue on a glass jar.

2 Press a length of wool on to the glue to make the outline of a snail.

3 Fill in the outline by coiling the wool towards the centre. Then cut off the extra wool.

**4** Repeat, using the other shapes shown. Press the strands of wool closely together so that no glass shows.

**5** Leave to dry.

**6** Fill in the spaces between the shapes in the same way. Continue until the whole jar is covered.

4 – 5.

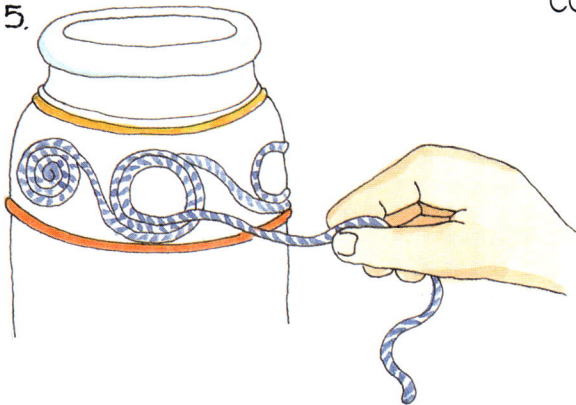

6.

## To make Christmas decorations.

Smear an inflated balloon with Vaseline. Cut 30cm lengths of string. Dip them into the glue, then wind round the balloon.

Hang to dry.

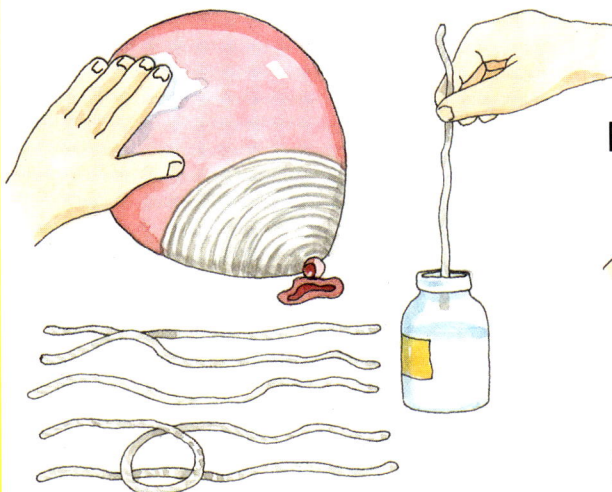

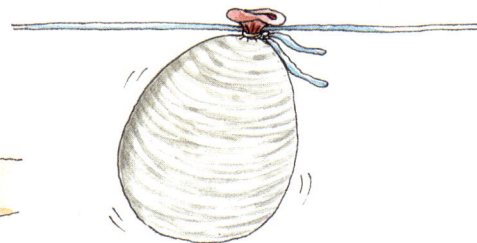

Burst the balloon.

Paint the ball gold or silver.

# FABRIC PAINTING

Make you own designer vest or T-shirt and impress your friends.

**You will need:**

card
fabric paints/brushes
black felt pen
iron and clean cloth
pins
T-shirt or vest

CAUTION: irons can be dangerous. Ask an adult to help you make this item.

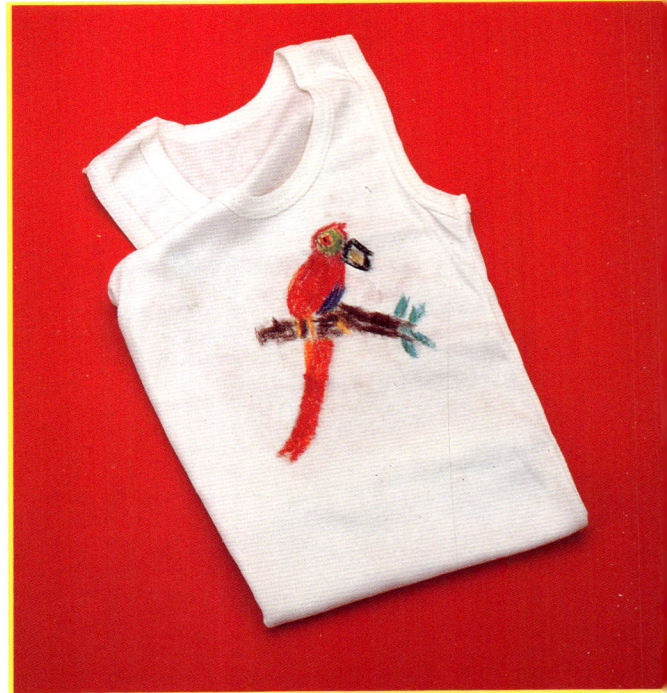

**1** Take a piece of card smaller than the front of your T-shirt.

**2** Draw your design on to the card using a black felt pen.

1.

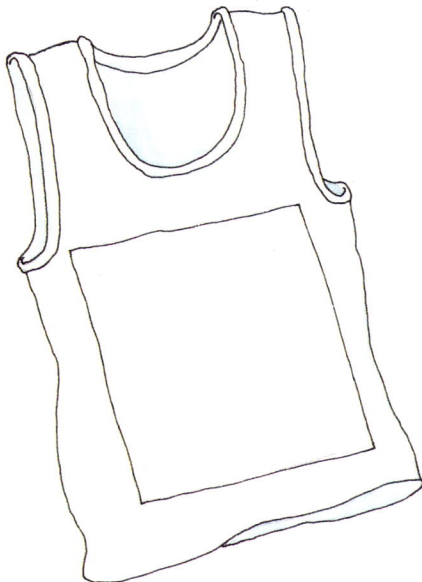

2.

3.

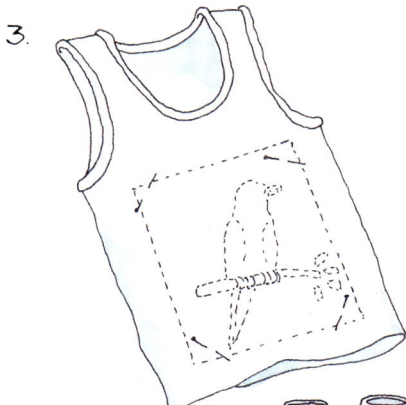

**3** Place the card inside the T-shirt so that the design shows through the front. Pin into place.

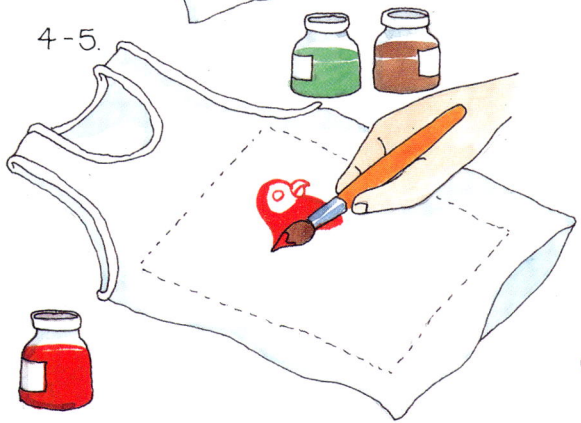

**4** Carefully paint your picture. Use thick paint, applying it with short strokes or dabs.

4 - 5.

**5** Leave to dry.

**6** Remove the card, then cover with a clean cloth and iron.

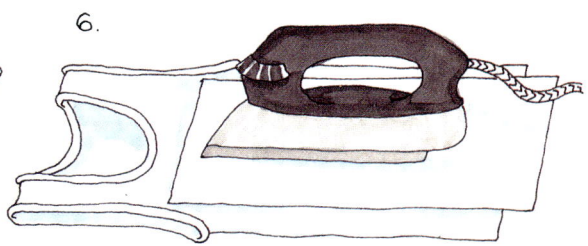

6.

Designs painted on small squares of material can be used as patches, or to decorate a bag.

# PLANT POT HOLDER

This plant pot holder is made by tying knots in the twine. Decorative knotting like this is called macramé.

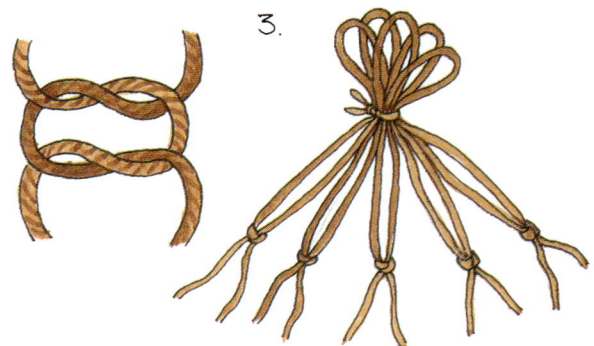

1.

**1** Cut the twine into five lengths of 180cm each.

**2** Fold in half and tie 5cm from the top.

**3** Separate the lengths of twine into pairs and knot them in a row, 10cm from the tie.

2.

3.

**4** Take a piece of twine from each knot and make another row of knots 5cm below.

**5** Make two more rows, each 5cm apart.

**6** Tie all the pieces together in an overhand knot as shown.

overhand knot

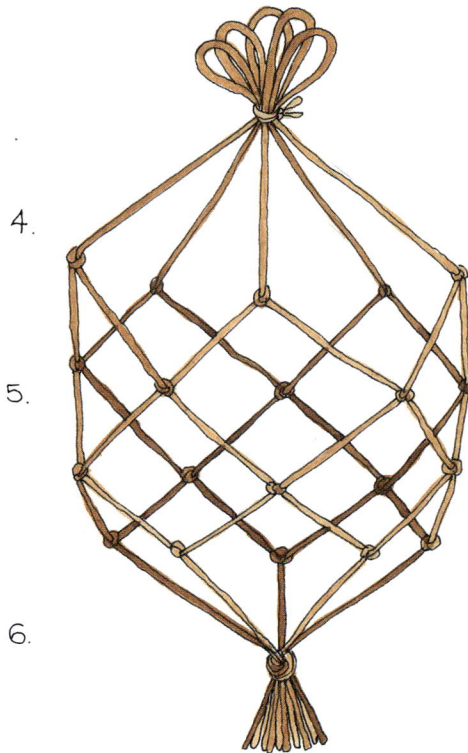

4.

5.

6.

## Wall Hanging

Cut twelve slits along the top and bottom of a piece of card.

Wind a length of wool round the card, through the slits.

Weave pieces of rag through the wool. Tie the ends together in pairs.

# POP-UP PUPPET

Pop-up puppets are great fun and make highly original presents.

**You will need:**

bamboo cane
card
  (20cm × 30cm)
cotton
fabric pens
glue

material
needle
pencil
scissors
stuffing
wool

1.

2.

3.

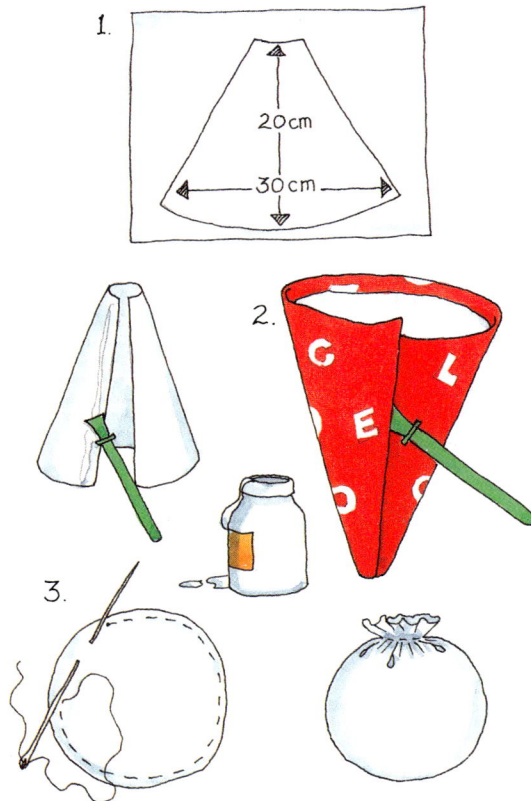

1 Cut out a piece of card in the shape shown. Use it as a template to cut the material.

2 Glue the two edges of the card together to make a cone shape. Cover with the material, sticking the edges down firmly.

3 Cut out a circle of light coloured material for a head. Sew running stitches round the edge. Pull the thread to make a bag. Fill with stuffing and fasten the cotton, leaving a small gap for the stick.

**4** Cut out 2 pieces of material in the shape shown, then cut out 2 felt hands. Stitch up the sides of the material and over the hands as shown.

**5** Push the stick into the bottom of the head, then lay between the two pieces of material and stitch across the top as shown. Sew the body to the head.

**6** Cut strands of wool for hair and sew them to the head.

**7** Draw on a mouth and eyes using a fabric pen.

**8** Push the stick through the cone and stitch the bottom of the puppet to the top of the cone.

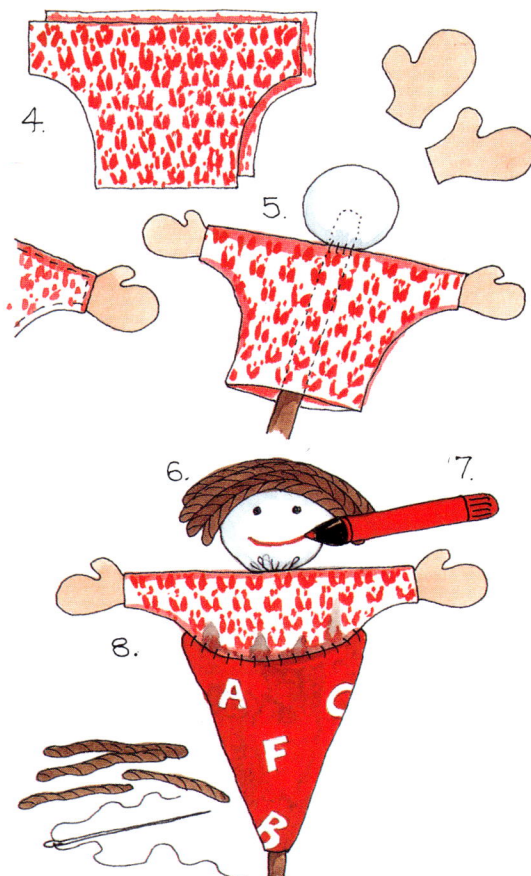

To make a glove puppet, cut out these shapes from material. Stitch as shown.

# BOOK LIST

If you want more ideas for practical craft activities the following books may be of interest. Your local library should be able to get copies for you.

Coleman, Anne.
**FABRICS AND YARNS**
*Wayland, 1989.*              1852106743
A book from the 'Craft Projects' series which has step by step drawings to show how materials can be used for a range of imaginative projects.

Devonshire, Hilary.
**COLLAGE**
*Franklin Watts, 1988.*      0863137091
A range of collage ideas which includes use of cork, sand, wool, fabric and paper. Also gives some ideas on how to mix these materials in one picture.

Hart, Tony.
**MAKING TREASURE**
*Kaye & Ward, 1983.*         071822955X
The most simple of craft books showing how to make gold coins, jewellery and a treasure chest; all from household materials. A slim volume with simple ideas.

Lancaster, John.
**CARD**
*Franklin Watts, 1989.*      0863138063
A lavishly illustrated book with some intricate sculptures. Helpful sections on scoring and bending card.

Pitcher, Caroline.
**ANIMALS**
*Franklin Watts, 1983.*      0863130437
How to make cows, snakes, dogs, hedgehogs and many more creatures, from things that are found in most homes and classrooms. Instructions for the projects are given by illustrations and there is not much written description.

Roussel, Mike.
**CLAY**
*Wayland, 1989.*             185210533X
A well-illustrated book on clay modelling with simple instructions covering various techniques from solid shaped models to pinch pots and coiling.

## For older children

Curtis, Annabelle, and Hindley, Judy.
**THE KNOW HOW BOOK OF PAPER FUN**
*Usborne, 1975.*             0860200000
A successful collection of things to make from paper and card in which the easiest ideas are at the beginning. It covers pop-up cards and mobiles as well as the more complex crocodile marionettes and a Jack-in-the-box.

Potter, Tony.
**POTTERY**
*Usborne, 1985.*             0860209458
A book which gives some detail about how clay can be used, but which does not necessarily involve much equipment. Plenty of ideas for a multitude of projects.

# INDEX